Original title:

Obsidian Whispers Inside the Fae Cowl

Author: Paula Raudsepp

ISBN HARDBACK: 978-1-80562-529-2

ISBN PAPERBACK: 978-1-80564-050-9

Threads of Light in the Gloom

In shadows deep, where whispers tread,
A flicker glows, a hope unsaid.
Through tangled paths, the dreams await,
To guide the lost beyond their fate.

With every spark, a story weaves,
A tapestry of hearts that cleaves.
In darkest hours, we find the way,
As threads of light lead night to day.

Secrets Beneath Mossy Canopies

Beneath the boughs of emerald gloom,
Where ancient tales entwine and bloom.
The forest whispers, soft and low,
Of secrets wrapped in twilight's glow.

In every leaf a story stirs,
Of lost loves written in the furs.
The mossy floors hold whispers tight,
Revealing dreams in muted light.

The Dance of Dimmed Luminescence

When twilight casts her silken spell,
The stars arise with tales to tell.
They twirl and spin in moonlit grace,
A dance of shadows, a soft embrace.

Each flicker hides a world once known,
In silence, memories are sown.
The dimmed light guides the weary home,
In night's sweet arms, no more to roam.

Riddles Spun from Night's Embrace

In mystic hours where silence reigns,
The night unfolds her hidden chains.
With starlit riddles wrapped in dreams,
The moonlight whispers, softly gleams.

Each question posed in hazy hue,
Invites the heart to seek the true.
In shadows deep, the answers lie,
As night unveils the waking sky.

Enigmatic Play of Light and Dark

In shadows deep, the secrets lie,
A flicker bright, a whispered sigh.
The dance of dusk, where dreams ignite,
And stars conspire with soft twilight.

With every flicker, stories twine,
The edges blurred, where worlds combine.
In silence deep, the echoes play,
A canvas brushed with night and day.

Stories Carried on the Night Breeze

The night unfolds, a tale untold,
In whispered breaths, the dreams unfold.
Through winding paths and ancient trees,
The stories ride on evening's breeze.

From starlit skies to shadowed glens,
The echoes call of olden friends.
Each gust a memory, soft and clear,
A symphony that all can hear.

The Enchanted Realm's Soft Embrace

In every nook, the magic weaves,
As moonlight dances, softly cleaves.
The gentle touch, a lover's grace,
In twilight's realm, we find our place.

With ivy twined and blossoms bright,
The world transforms in deepening night.
A heartbeat found in every path,
Where nature sings its flowing wrath.

Reflections in Moonlit Waters

The silver sheen on tranquil lakes,
Where every ripple softly wakes.
Beneath the stars, the dreams take flight,
In mirrored depths, the heart's delight.

A tapestry of dark and light,
The water's whispers, pure and slight.
In stillness held, the secrets dwell,
Where magic breathes, and shadows swell.

Fae Light and the Dance of Hidden Paths

In shadows deep, where secrets dwell,
The fae lights flicker, cast their spell.
A dance begins on whispering grass,
With every heartbeat, moments pass.

Through twisted trees and moonlight gleam,
A hidden path leads to a dream.
The laughter echoes, soft and bright,
Guiding lost souls with pure delight.

Soft petals flutter, in twilight's fold,
A tale of magic, waiting to be told.
With every step, enchantments weave,
A dance of wonders, if you believe.

The laughter mingles with the night,
Stars above, a shimmering sight.
Twilight holds its breath in awe,
Nature's secret, a hidden law.

So follow the glow, let your heart sway,
In fae light's embrace, forever stay.
Through hidden paths, find your song,
In the dance of dreams, you belong.

The Secrets Beneath the Faery Arch

Beneath the arch where faeries play,
Lies a world where shadows stray.
Whispered giggles, silvery light,
Guide curious hearts through the night.

Secrets slumber in ancient stone,
In every nook, magic is sown.
With every breeze, mysteries sigh,
Calling the brave who dare to try.

In twilight's haze, the lanterns gleam,
Casting spells like a waking dream.
The lost and found converge at dusk,
Morning's chill is a warming hush.

As starlight dances on the dew,
Stories unfold for the chosen few.
Beneath the arch, time will bend,
An adventure that never ends.

Embrace the wonder, heed the lore,
Within the faery secrets, explore.
With open hearts and spirits free,
Discover magic's tapestry.

Dreamweaver's Lullaby in the Gloom

In the hush of night, where shadows play,
A dreamweaver hums her soft array.
Lullabies whisper through the trees,
Carried gently on the breeze.

Stars blink above, like watchful eyes,
Mapping out the dusky skies.
In the gloom, hopes intertwine,
As dreams unfurl their silken line.

Through the mist, a soft caress,
A promise wraps in tenderness.
Each note a balm for weary souls,
Restoring hearts, making them whole.

The night brings tales of distant lands,
Where wishes bloom in gentle hands.
With every sigh, the world takes flight,
In the embrace of the velvet night.

Awake, dear child, in dreams engage,
The dreamweaver turns the page.
In the lull of dark, your spirit flies,
To realms unseen beyond the skies.

Tales Whispers of the Moonlit Marsh

In the marsh where shadows cling,
Whispers weave like a gentle string.
Moonlight dances on silvery reeds,
Telling tales of forgotten deeds.

The croon of frogs, the rustling breeze,
Nature's chorus, a soft unease.
Amongst the gloom, mysteries bloom,
A tapestry spun in twilight's room.

With every step, the stories grow,
Of faeries hiding, long ago.
Spectres sway in the misty night,
Guarding secrets hidden from sight.

Watch the ripples in the cool dark,
Each a echo, each a spark.
Voices murmur on the pond's edge,
Where magical stories pledge.

Lost in the woods, hear the call,
The marsh holds wonders for one and all.
Through moonlit paths, your heart shall soar,
In fae's embrace, you'll find much more.

Gossamer Threads of Hidden Realms

In shadows dance the whispers light,
Through dreams that shimmer, soft and bright.
A tapestry of worlds concealed,
Where truths and fables are revealed.

With every thread, a tale is spun,
Of ancient forests, skies that run.
Through tangled paths, the secret calls,
From hidden realms where magic sprawls.

In silver breezes, secrets glide,
On gossamer wings, they will not hide.
With laughter born from airy sighs,
In veils of myths, the wonder lies.

The moonlit dance of fairies fair,
In corners lost, we find them there.
Gossamer threads entwined with fate,
In worlds beyond, they softly wait.

So close your eyes, embrace the night,
Let whispers guide you to their light.
For in those realms, we'll find our way,
A journey woven, come what may.

Whispering Leaves and Silent Stars

Beneath the boughs where shadows play,
The leaves converse in soft ballet.
They share the tales of times long past,
Where secrets linger, shadows cast.

The silent stars, they twinkle bright,
In velvet skies, a wondrous sight.
Each one a wish, each twinkle a dream,
In quiet nights, they softly gleam.

The rustling leaves, they speak of fate,
Of ancient woods, and paths ornate.
From dusk till dawn, the stories hum,
With nature's heartbeat, we succumb.

In whispered tones, the night unfolds,
A symphony of life retold.
When hearts are still, and worries cease,
The darkness wraps us in its peace.

So let us wander, hand in hand,
Through whispering leaves, a magic land.
With silent stars, our hopes align,
In nature's depths, our souls entwine.

Beneath the Cloak of Darkness

In twilight's arms, the shadows creep,
A world awakens from its sleep.
Beneath the cloak where dreams may rest,
The heart finds solace, gently pressed.

The nightingale sings a lullaby,
As stars emerge in the velvet sky.
Each note a promise, pure and true,
In moonlight's glow, we start anew.

With every breath, the stillness grows,
In silent woods, where magic flows.
The whispers of the ancient trees,
Carry tales on the evening breeze.

Through hidden paths, the shadows call,
A murmur soft like a lover's thrall.
In darkness deep, the spirits play,
A ballet grand, in night's soft sway.

So journey forth, with heart aglow,
Through realms unknown, let passions flow.
For in the cloak that night bestows,
The secrets of the universe grow.

Secrets Woven in Twilight

When twilight whispers to the day,
And colors merge in soft array.
On threads of light, the secrets weave,
In every heart, they nest and leave.

The sun dips low, the stars arise,
As moonbeams dance through painted skies.
In every shadow, stories lie,
Of journeys taken, yet to fly.

Softly now, the magic glows,
In twilight's hue, the wonder flows.
Each moment rich with dreams untold,
A tapestry of life unfolds.

With every breath, a spark ignites,
In twinkling stars, our hopes take flight.
Through woven paths of dusk and dawn,
The heartbeat of the night goes on.

So take a step into the night,
Let twilight's secrets guide your flight.
Through layers soft, and shadows deep,
In twilight's weave, our souls shall leap.

Whispers from the Realm of Shadows

In the stillness where secrets weave,
Shadows dance, and whispers breathe.
Ancient echoes call the brave,
Through the darkness, a path to pave.

Ghostly figures flicker and sway,
Guardians of night, they softly play.
With every breath, a story spun,
Of battles lost and victories won.

A flicker of light, a fleeting glance,
Entwined in shadows, the spirits prance.
From the depths, a haunting song,
Sings of places where dreams belong.

Cloaked in mystery, they bind and weave,
Promises of wonders that hearts believe.
If you dare, step through the veil,
Into the realm where whispers sail.

For in the shadows, truth does lie,
Waiting patiently, giving a sigh.
The night reveals, if you just see,
The magic that whispers, wild and free.

Glistening Nightfall Beneath Starlit Myths

Glistening nightfall whispers low,
Underneath a blanket of starlit glow.
Myths awaken in the silver light,
Carried forth on wings of night.

Dreams take flight on a midnight breeze,
Dancing softly through whispering trees.
Echoes of stories long untold,
Beneath the sky, a treasure of gold.

Oh, moonlit paths where fairies tread,
Laughter echoes where hopes are fed.
A tapestry woven with threads of fate,
Inviting wanderers to navigate.

Stars align, their shimmer bright,
Guiding hearts in the velvet night.
In this realm where time stands still,
Magic whispers, and dreams fulfill.

So breathe the night, let spirits soar,
For in this place, you'll seek and explore.
With every twinkle, a story spins,
In the starlit tales where adventure begins.

The Allure of Hidden Mysteries

Beneath the surface, a world unknown,
Whispers of truths that have overgrown.
In shadows deep, secrets reside,
Waiting patiently, with nowhere to hide.

The allure of mysteries calls to the brave,
Enticing hearts, a treasure to save.
With quiet steps, the curious tread,
Into the depths, where wonders spread.

Stories linger in the air so thick,
Calling to seekers, both gentle and quick.
The hidden paths twist and twine,
Leading to places where stars align.

Each mystery layered like pages in books,
Awaiting the gaze of inquisitive looks.
Embrace the unknown, let your heart roam,
In the allure of shadows, you'll find your home.

As the sun bows low, the night unfolds,
Unraveling tales of the brave and the bold.
The curious souls who dare to seek,
Shall unearth the truths that nature speaks.

Veils of Twilight's Enchantment

Twilight dances on the edge of day,
Casting shadows where the lost dreams play.
Veils of enchantment softly draw near,
Wrapping the world in a tender veneer.

Colors bleed in the evening light,
Painting the heavens, a wondrous sight.
Each moment drips with a magic rare,
Inviting whispers into the air.

Listen closely to the sighing breeze,
As twilight beckons through the trees.
In this realm, where illusions blend,
Time holds its breath, around each bend.

A flicker of starlight, a shimmer of gold,
Stories of old, waiting to be told.
Lift the veil of the dusky hue,
And find the enchantment meant for you.

So wander gently 'neath the twilight's glow,
Let every breath your heart bestow.
In this magical hour, let dreams ignite,
For within the veils, lies a world of light.

Lanterns of Lore Beneath the Boughs

In twilight's glow, the lanterns dance,
Their flickering lights, a fleeting chance.
Old stories whisper through the leaves,
Echoes of magic that the night weaves.

Ancient owls with wise, knowing eyes,
Guard fragile dreams beneath the skies.
The heart of the woods sings soft and low,
With secrets that only the moonlit know.

Branches entwine like fingers in prayer,
Cradling the wonders hidden with care.
A tapestry woven with threads of past,
Holding the sorrows, joys that will last.

Each rustle and sigh fills the air with lore,
While shadows stretch, beckoning more.
A pathway of whispers leads through the night,
Illuminated softly by the gentle light.

The Glyphs of the Forest Floor

Beneath the trees, where shadows play,
Lie secrets etched in earth's ballet.
Glyphs of old, in silence they glean,
Tales of the woodland, ages unseen.

Each footprint tells a story deep,
Of wanderers lost in tranquil sleep.
Moss-covered stones hold wisdom true,
In every curve, in every hue.

Where roots intertwine, a message is shown,
A language of life in green overgrown.
From ferns that whisper to flowers that cry,
The forest speaks softly, beneath the sky.

Hasten not, for time here flows slow,
Understanding the rhythm of ebb and glow.
With careful hands, tread lightly, my friend,
The glyphs of the forest invite you to mend.

Secrets Lurking in the Gloom

In shadows thick, where the cold winds roam,
Lurk ancient secrets far from home.
Hidden in graves of crumbling stone,
Tales of the forgotten, left all alone.

Mists shroud the path, thick with despair,
As creatures of night with potent glare
Guard the enchantments held in their grip,
Waiting for daring souls to unzip.

Echoes of laughter, sharp and clear,
Spin tales of joy now tainted by fear.
A dance of spirits, lost and bereaved,
In the depths of the night, hearts grieved.

To wander here is to flirt with the fates,
Where darkness entices and nothing awaits.
You'll find a riddle etched in the gloom,
A glimpse of light, in shadows' womb.

Whispers of the Sylvan Spirits

In woods alive with murmurs of grace,
The sylvan spirits weave through the space.
With laughter like chimes and voices like streams,
They cradle the forest in sweet-scented dreams.

A flicker of light, a rustle of leaves,
An echo that dances and gently weaves.
Each breeze carries stories of joy and pain,
Of love that lingers like dew after rain.

The trees sway with wisdom, roots deeply sown,
Guardians of secrets, eternally grown.
From twilight's cloak to the dawn's first sigh,
Whispers of spirits linger and fly.

In the heart of the woods, all spirits commune,
Casting their blessings beneath the moon.
For in every rustle, in every breath,
The whispers of nature speak love and death.

Riddles of the Haunted Grove

In shadows deep where whispers dwell,
The trees stand tall, and secrets swell.
Through winding paths, the spirits glide,
Their ancient tales the night'll confide.

Beneath the moon, a silver veil,
A haunting tune begins to wail.
The flickering lights, they beckon near,
To unravel truths long held dear.

Cold winds whisper with a sigh,
Lost dreams drift like clouds on high.
Each rustle and each sighing breeze,
Hides tales of woe beneath the leaves.

A lantern flickers in the haze,
Guiding the lost through twilight's maze.
Beneath the boughs of ancient lore,
Lies the key to what's before.

Echoes linger, wrapped in time,
Cryptic clues and riddles rhyme.
As dawn breaks through with gentle light,
Will you embrace the coming night?

Twilight's Lament in the Sylvan Depths

The twilight sighs, a gentle breath,
As shadows dance, and whispers death.
In leafy arms where secrets weave,
The trees lament what they believe.

With every sigh of evening's bliss,
A longing pulse in nature's kiss.
The glowing stars begin to peep,
As dreams awaken from their sleep.

O wandering souls, with burdened hearts,
To find the light where darkness parts.
In sylvan depths, the echoes call,
To seek what's lost, and rise or fall.

A flicker of hope in shadows gray,
Guides the weary on their way.
The branches stretch, like arms to clasp,
In twilight's charm, the moments grasp.

Yet in this grove of whispered tales,
A sorrow flows where sunlight fails.
Will you depart, or choose to stay
And join the night where shadows play?

The Enigma of Fae's Breath

In glades where sunlight doesn't reach,
The Fae weave spells beyond our speech.
With laughter borne on fragrant air,
They guard the woods with tender care.

Each dewdrop holds a secret bright,
A world unseen, a glimmering light.
Beware the thorns that softly glow,
For faerie folk may steal a woe.

Through flickering fireflies' flight,
Their laughter twinkling in the night.
What dreams they weave within your sleep,
The cost of joy may cut so deep.

In twilight's hush, their whispers play,
A riddle cloaked in bright array.
With every glance, the shadows bend,
Will you break free, or will you mend?

To seek the truth in hidden glades,
Is to embrace the Fae's charades.
In echoes soft, their magic's strength,
Will turn the night at last to length.

Echoes of Charmed Nightwalkers

In moonlit hours when darkness swirls,
The nightwalkers weave their pearls.
With every step, a story flows,
In silver threads the magic grows.

Their laughter echoes through the trees,
A haunting serenade on the breeze.
With glinting eyes, they watch and wait,
To unveil secrets locked by fate.

With shadows dancing in their wake,
They tread the paths where few hearts ache.
In fleeting dreams, they beckon near,
To chase the stars, to face the fear.

A flicker here, a shimmer there,
In every corner, magic's glare.
What wonders lie beyond the night,
When heart and soul take flight, take flight?

But tread with care, for they are sly,
With whispered charms, they know the why.
In echoes faint, you hold the key,
To enter realms where you are free.

Murmured Musings of Sylvan Lore

In twilight's grasp where whispers dwell,
The ancient trees weave tales to tell.
Beneath the boughs, the soft winds sigh,
As secrets linger in the sky.

With every rustle, stories rise,
Of hidden realms beneath the skies.
A brook babbles, a lullaby,
Where dreams drift gently, low and high.

The stars above blink in delight,
A dance of fireflies ignites the night.
Nature's musings in colors bright,
Painting the dusk with pure delight.

In shadows deep, the echoes call,
The sylvan spirits, one and all.
In every leaf, a magic spun,
A testament of earth, and sun.

So come, dear friend, and heed the lore,
Of sylvan whispers, evermore.
For in this wood, hearts intertwine,
And soul and nature both align.

Fae's Serenade in Silent Pines

In stillness wrapped, the pines do sway,
As fae embark on night's ballet.
With laughter soft, like streams that flow,
They twirl and dance in moonlit glow.

Each leaf a stage, each branch a dream,
Their voices rise like crystal stream.
A serenade that lifts the night,
In shadows deep, the world's delight.

With silver wings, they dip and dive,
In every breeze, the magic thrives.
Their melodies, a soothing balm,
Transform the dark with gentle calm.

Through whispered trees, the stories weave,
Of love and loss, and hearts that grieve.
Yet joy is found in fleeting flight,
As fae embrace the whispered night.

So let us wander, hand in hand,
Through scented glades, a timeless land.
Where fae and dreams forever dwell,
In pines where secrets rise and swell.

The Dance of Shadows and Light

In twilight hues, the shadows play,
With gentle grace, they drift away.
A waltz of dusk and dawn entwined,
Where flickers of fate are often blind.

In golden rays, the laughter peeks,
While silver mist in silence speaks.
Each moment caught, a fleeting bliss,
As day and night share a stolen kiss.

The path unfurls with softest tread,
Where light and shadow dare to wed.
A tapestry, both bright and bleak,
In every corner, mysteries seek.

Yet in the depths of darkest space,
A beacon shines with hopeful grace.
For every gloom, a spark ignites,
In endless cycles of days and nights.

So dance we shall, with heart in hand,
In realms where dreams and shadows stand.
For in this waltz, both lost and found,
Life's rhythm pulses, soft and profound.

Lore of the Undergrowth's Heart

Beneath the canopy, humble and sparse,
Lies the undergrowth, a vibrant farce.
Where moss blankets earth in verdant hue,
And secrets hide in the morning dew.

The creatures scurry, in shadows reside,
With whispers soft that the leaves confide.
A melody, earthy and rich, resounds,
In every nook, adventure abounds.

From ancient roots, the stories flow,
Of battles fought and hearts that glow.
Where time doth linger, wrapped in embrace,
Nature's tapestry, a sacred space.

In thickets thick, the tales converge,
Of kin and kinship, a silent surge.
The pulse of life, a timeless beat,
In the undergrowth's heart where spirits meet.

So wander forth, with reverent grace,
To uncover the lore in this hidden place.
Embrace the whispers, the tales untold,
For in the wild, life's magic unfolds.

The Allure of Twilight's Embrace

As shadows dance on ancient stone,
The stars awaken, whispers grown.
In twilight's glow, a secret we weave,
A world of magic, ready to believe.

The breeze carries tales from days of yore,
Of heroes and dreams, of legends and lore.
In each soft sigh, a promise laid,
Of warmth and wonder, unafraid.

The moon hangs low, a silver thread,
Connecting hearts where dreams are fed.
In the hush, we find our place,
Embraced by night's enchanting grace.

Every shadow paints a story bright,
With colors spun from the fabric of night.
In the glow of dusk, our spirits rise,
Bound by the magic of endless skies.

So let us linger, time stands still,
In twilight's embrace, we drink our fill.
Of stardust dreams and whispered lore,
In this sacred hour, forevermore.

Lanterns of Lore in a Forgotten Glade

Softly glowing, lanterns sway,
Guiding wanderers lost in their way.
In a glade where stories sleep,
Ancient secrets dive so deep.

Whispers of trees, a rustling song,
Calling forth the brave and strong.
Beneath the boughs, where shadows twine,
Lives a magic, pure and divine.

Crickets chirp in evening's hush,
As hearts race wild in the twilight rush.
With every step on the mossy floor,
They uncover the tales of folklore.

Glimmers of hope in amber light,
Guide the lost through the starry night.
With each flicker, a story unfurls,
Of knights and quests from forgotten worlds.

So gather, friends, where lanterns gleam,
In the deep woods, ignite the dream.
With open hearts, embrace the lore,
In this forgotten glade, forevermore.

Silent Currents of Enchanted Realms

Beneath the waves of moonlit tide,
Silent currents hold secrets beside.
In enchanted realms, where whispers roam,
The heart finds solace, a watery home.

Ripples carry tales of the deep,
Where mermaids sing and secrets sleep.
With every swirl, the past unfolds,
A treasure trove of dreams untold.

Veils of mist shroud the waiting dawn,
In currents soft, the magic's drawn.
Each wave a story, each tide a song,
In the dance of shadows, we all belong.

From ocean's depths to the stars above,
In silent currents, we learn to love.
In quiet moments, we discover why,
The heart of magic will never die.

So let us sail where the moonlight spills,
And seek the magic that time distills.
In enchanted realms, our spirits rise,
Forever bound beneath starlit skies.

Veiled Faces in the Whispering Wood

In the whispering wood, shadows play,
Veiled faces linger, night and day.
With each rustle, a story calls,
Eclipsing the sun as twilight falls.

They gather close, in robes woven tight,
Guardians of secrets, cloaked in night.
In their silence, wisdom shared,
With every glance, a heart laid bare.

The moon's soft glow reveals their grace,
In this hidden land, we find our place.
With laughter ringing, spirits soar,
In the embrace of the woods' folklore.

As leaves convene in the gentle breeze,
Veiled faces smile; they aim to please.
In the shadows, echoes of the past,
In this hushed haven, memories last.

So tread with care where mysteries lie,
In the whispering wood, under starry sky.
For veiled faces watch, their stories reside,
In the secret depths where dreams collide.

The Enigma of Silken Darkness

In shadows deep the whispers weave,
A tale of night that none believe.
With threads of silk, the dark unfolds,
Mysteries wrapped, in silence holds.

A lantern's glow, a fading sigh,
Hints of the lost that linger nigh.
Where secrets hide, in veils so grand,
The enigma breathes, slips through our hand.

In velvet cloaks the phantoms prance,
With every step, a haunting dance.
The stars above, like watchful eyes,
Gleam down upon the quiet lies.

Yet courage stirs within the heart,
To piece together every part.
And though the dark may seem a foe,
It teaches us what we must know.

For woven dreams in silence dwell,
In secret realms where shadows swell.
To face the night, the soul must dare,
To find the light that lingers there.

Beneath the Gaze of Celestial Guardians

Beneath the stars that shine in grace,
A world awakes in soft embrace.
The guardians of the night so bright,
Watch over dreams that take their flight.

In silver beams, the whispers flow,
Through fields that glisten, hearts aglow.
With every wish upon the breeze,
The stars align with playful ease.

The moonlight bathes the earth in glow,
While shadows dance, and hopes bestow.
A serenade of lost desires,
Ignites the spark of hidden fires.

Celestial dreams in stillness rest,
As night enfolds our fervent quest.
With every heartbeat, every sigh,
We reach for worlds beyond the sky.

For in the gaze of watchful eyes,
We find the truth that never dies.
And through the night, we shall ascend,
The journey's end, a magical blend.

Whispers from the Forgotten Woodlands

In ancient groves where secrets dwell,
The echoes weave their mystic spell.
Beneath the boughs where shadows sigh,
Whispers emerge as stars slip by.

The rustling leaves sing tales untold,
Of love once lost, of hearts so bold.
Each step reveals the paths of old,
Where dreams are sewn, and time unfolds.

Through tangled vines and twilight's breath,
Life's memories dance, defying death.
With gentle grace, the forest calls,
To wanderers drawn to its hallowed halls.

In fading light, the magic thrums,
As stories linger, and silence hums.
The woodlands speak, their spirits near,
In every shadow, wisdom's cheer.

So heed the calls that echo wide,
In forgotten woods where dreams abide.
With open heart and eager mind,
The whispers guide, true magic find.

The Lure of Veiled Enchantment

In twilight hours where secrets gleam,
The air is thick with whispered dream.
Veils of enchantment smooth the way,
Inviting souls to lose their sway.

A twilight dance 'neath shimmering skies,
Where every gaze ignites surprise.
The heartbeats quicken, pulses race,
For magic stirs in this embrace.

With every step through misty glades,
The promise lingers, never fades.
A world anew in shadows cast,
Where present meets the echoes past.

The spark of wonder fills the night,
As starlit paths unfold in light.
With every whisper, dare to dream,
For life is never what it seems.

So follow where the veils entwine,
And let your spirit's essence shine.
In every glance and fleeting chance,
Find magic's lure, and dare to dance.

The Echoing Silence of the Night

In shadows deep where secrets dwell,
The stars above weave tales to tell.
A hush envelopes all around,
In night's embrace, no other sound.

The whispers of the ancient trees,
Bring forth the magic with gentle breeze.
Moonlight dances on silver streams,
Cradling softly our hidden dreams.

Yet in this silence, echoes rise,
Of laughter lost and silent cries.
A tapestry of what once was,
In stillness, hear the world's applause.

Each heartbeat echoes in the dark,
Woven tales, a fragile spark.
In night's embrace, we bow our heads,
To the stories sung by stars like threads.

The silence speaks in volumes clear,
Of love and loss, of hope and fear.
When all is quiet, all is bright,
In the echoing silence of the night.

Journey Through the Lost Thicket

Through thickets thick where shadows cling,
A path unfolds, adventure's ring.
With every step, the whispers call,
Enticing souls to heed their thrall.

Among the trees, the secrets twine,
A map of dreams in ivy vine.
Each bramble holds a tale untold,
Of hidden glens and treasures bold.

The air is rich with ancient lore,
As spirits of the woods explore.
They beckon kindred hearts to stray,
Through winding paths that fade away.

In lost thickets where fairies dwell,
An echo rings of magic's spell.
With every turn, the heart does race,
In this enchanted, wild embrace.

Together we'll weave paths anew,
In the thicket, wild and true.
With nature's guide, we'll make our mark,
Joyful souls igniting sparks.

Fables Spun from Moonlit Threads

In silver beams, the stories flow,
Of whispered winds and soft moon glow.
Each fable spun from threads of night,
Is woven deep in dreams' soft light.

The owl sings songs of ages past,
Each note a spell, each word a cast.
Under the watchful moon's embrace,
We find the truth in time and space.

Through twilight's veil, the shadows dance,
With gentle grace, they take their chance.
To wander free through stories old,
As fables bright in dreams unfold.

With every tale, a spark ignites,
A beacon calling through the nights.
From ancient times to futures near,
We grasp the magic, hold it dear.

In moonlit threads, our hopes align,
Through fables bound by stars that shine.
With heart in hand, we journey far,
A tapestry of who we are.

The Allure of the Midnight Wood

In midnight wood, where shadows creep,
Secrets linger, promises keep.
The call of night, an echo sweet,
Inviting all to take their seat.

Beneath the boughs, the world stands still,
A haunting dance, a gentle thrill.
The moon hangs low, a watchful eye,
As whispers weave and spirits fly.

With every rustle, stories wake,
Of paths once walked and dreams at stake.
In the allure of twilight's embrace,
We seek the light, we chase its grace.

Through wooded halls where mysteries roam,
A heart finds peace; a place called home.
In tangled roots, our fears subside,
As midnight wood becomes our guide.

In every shadow, there's a spark,
A guiding light in realms so dark.
With midnight hues and starlit skies,
The wood calls forth our truth, our rise.

Silhouettes in the Forest of Echoes

In twilight's grasp, the shadows play,
Dancing figures drift away,
Whispers swirl through ancient trees,
A melody on furtive breeze.

Mossy carpets cloaked in gloom,
Glimmers spark with hints of doom,
Footsteps tread on echoes lost,
A haunting song at nature's cost.

Stars awaken, twinkling bright,
Guiding lost souls through the night,
Beneath branches bowed and bent,
Lives a world of whispered intent.

Secrets linger in the air,
Tales untold, a patient stare,
The forest breathes with every sigh,
As shadows weave and softly lie.

Yet in this realm where spirits dwell,
Beauty blooms, though darkness fell,
Through echoes, hear the gentle call,
In the forest, we are all.

Release the fears that cloud your mind,
In the silhouettes, peace you'll find,
For every whisper, every sigh,
Holds a truth that never dies.

Murmurs of the Veiled Spirits

In moonlit groves, the shadows weave,
Soft murmurs rise, like whispers leave,
Veils of mist that cloak the night,
Where spirits stir in silvery light.

Each breath a prayer, each sigh a song,
In the dark where they belong,
Echoing tales of lost delights,
Caught between the days and nights.

Their laughter dances on the air,
Elusive forms, a ghostly flair,
Beneath the branches, spirits play,
In the twilight's warm embrace, they stay.

Through swirling fog, their secrets twine,
A tapestry where shadows shine,
In the stillness, hearts may find,
Connection wrapped in threads entwined.

So pause a moment, listen near,
For every whisper held so dear,
The veiled spirits gently call,
In their realm, we are never small.

Beneath the Shroud of Darkness

Underneath the starless hue,
Where no light shines, yet dreams break through,
A world awaits both brave and lost,
Within the night's encroaching frost.

Wisps of shadows drift and sway,
Encasing fears that lead astray,
Yet in the gloom, there's beauty found,
If one can listen to the sound.

Through tangled paths where few have tread,
Memories linger of what is said,
A quiet strength in dark's embrace,
A promise held in silence' grace.

Night's cloak enfolds, yet hearts ignite,
With flickers of magic, bold and bright,
For every shade that hides away,
Holds a spark to light the day.

So venture forth with courage true,
Beneath the shroud, there's much to view,
For in the dark, the heart can see,
The countless paths that lead to free.

Serenade of the Enigmatic Night

In the stillness, whispers hum,
A serenade; the night's sweet drum,
Stars align, their twinkling light,
Guides lost dreams through endless night.

Echoes rise like phantom tunes,
Underneath the watchful moons,
They beckon forth the questing heart,
In shadows where the secrets part.

With every note, the dark sings low,
Tales of yore from long ago,
A canvas vast, where echoes meld,
Dreams and memories once compelled.

Enigmas carved in starlit beams,
Gentle breezes, haunting dreams,
The night, a keeper of the past,
In its embrace, the die is cast.

So close your eyes, let visions flow,
In the serenade, let your heart know,
That in the night, where shadows sway,
A world awaits—just drift away.

Masked Dances in the Gleaming Night

In silent halls where shadows play,
Masked figures swirl in the moon's soft ray.
Whispers of secrets drift through the air,
As stars above twinkle with a knowing stare.

Eyes concealed, yet hearts laid bare,
Each pirouette speaks of love and despair.
Glimmers of fate weave in and out,
In this enchanted ballroom, casting out doubt.

The music swells, a haunting refrain,
Tales of joy and sorrow blend with pain.
A fleeting touch, a lost embrace,
In this masked dance, we find our grace.

Time drifts softly on silken wings,
As laughter echoes and the night sings.
Beneath the masks, true selves unfold,
In the gleaming night, adventures untold.

When twilight fades, the magic remains,
As the ballroom still breathes with untold gains.
With dawn's first light, shadows retreat,
Leaving behind whispers, bittersweet.

Echoes of Unseen Realms

Beyond the veil where mortals tread,
Whispers linger, stories unsaid.
Echoes call from a distant shore,
Where dreams of wonder beckon for more.

In twilight's grasp, they weave and wane,
Fragments of laughter, shadows of pain.
Through hidden paths, they gently flow,
In the heart of the night, secrets to sow.

Starlight guides with a silvery thread,
Connecting the living with those who've fled.
A tapestry spun from love and loss,
In unseen realms, we cherish the gloss.

Here in the quiet, the echoes grow,
Songs of the past in the softening glow.
Each whispered tale, like wind through the leaves,
Reminds us of magic, the heart believes.

So linger a while, in this sacred space,
Embrace the unseen with warmth and grace.
For in every echo, a truth will unfold,
Revealing the warmth of the stories retold.

The Depths of Twilit Enchantment

In the dusk where shadows play deep,
Mysteries awaken from slumber and sleep.
The air thrums softly with magic unseen,
As twilight weaves dreams in shades of green.

Crickets hum softly, a serenade bright,
While the stars blink awake in the velvety night.
With each whispered wish carried by breeze,
The world of enchantment swells with ease.

Through tangled vines, paths twist and turn,
Where secrets of old ignite and burn.
A lantern flickers with ethereal light,
Illuminating wonders of the deep night.

Step lightly, dear soul, in this twilight muse,
For magic lies waiting, yours to peruse.
With hearts open wide, embrace the unknown,
In the depths of enchantment, you'll find your home.

So dance with the shadows, let laughter take flight,
In the embrace of this beautiful night.
With each fleeting moment, let wonder ignite,
In the depths of twilit enchantment, hold tight.

Chants of the Mysterious Night

Beneath the cloak of a star-speckled sky,
Soft murmurs of magic float and fly.
In the shadows, a symphony plays,
Chants of the night in a mystical phase.

The moon smiles down with a silver embrace,
Casting soft light in this enchanted space.
Night creatures gather, their voices entwined,
In rhythmic chants, the universe aligned.

Listen closely, to tales they unfold,
Of heroes and legends, both brave and bold.
In whispers and echoes, the stories take flight,
As dreams are reborn in the arms of the night.

With each passing breath, a spell is cast,
Carrying hopes of the present and past.
Through the silence, let your spirit ignite,
In the beautiful magic of the mysterious night.

So breathe in the wonder, and dance with delight,
For the world is alive in the embrace of the night.
In the chants of the dark, let your heart take flight,
And discover the magic hidden from sight.

Secrets Snared in the Dusk

In twilight's embrace, whispers glide,
The world holds its breath, secrets bide.
With shadows of dreams that flicker and sway,
The night steals the light, fading to gray.

Beneath the old oak, where shadows weave,
The thoughts of the heart find room to believe.
In the echo of silence, past stories unfold,
The secrets of dusk, like treasures, turned gold.

Misty Reveries of Forgotten Magic

In the hush of the morning, a soft mist flows,
Carrying tales where the wildflower grows.
Forgotten spells on the wind do dance,
Whispered enchantments that stir and entrance.

With each rising sun, a mystery stirs,
Awakening dreams that belong to the firs.
Through valleys of emerald and skies so wide,
The air is alive with magic, our guide.

Murmurs of Enchanted Twilight

As the sun dips low in the evening sky,
The twilight murmurs a soft, sweet sigh.
Stars awaken, like eyes blink anew,
Filling the heavens with shimmering dew.

Each moment is woven with threads of light,
Binding the world in enchantment's sight.
In the heart of the dusk, where dreams intertwine,
Magic unfolds like an ancient design.

Shadows in the Hollow Tree

In the heart of the forest, a hollowed old tree,
Holds secrets of centuries, wild and free.
Within its dark embrace, stories confide,
Of spirits and whispers, of love and of pride.

The shadows that linger, in twilight's soft glow,
Carry the dreams that are lost long ago.
With each gentle rustle, the past comes alive,
In shadows and silence, the memories thrive.

The Enchantment of the Ambient Shade

Beneath the whispering leaves, shadows dance,
Where secrets linger, a hidden romance.
The breeze sings softly, casting its spell,
In this enchanted glade, all is well.

Flickering lights, like stars up above,
Guide weary travelers, in search of love.
Each step reveals wonders, ancient and wise,
In the heart of the shade, where magic lies.

The wildflowers bloom in colors so bright,
Under the watch of the moon's gentle light.
Roots intertwine, a tapestry rare,
In the ambient shade, free from despair.

Echoes of laughter, the past comes alive,
In this sacred space, dreams start to thrive.
A tapestry woven with tales long untold,
In the warmth of the shade, let the soul unfold.

Secrets of the Gloomy Vale

In the vale where shadows creep,
Secrets murmur, old and deep.
Moonlit paths twist and twine,
Whispers of fate in the bramble's spine.

The mist embraces the ancient stones,
Guarding the secrets in hushed tones.
Graves of giants, remnants of yore,
Stirred by the winds, they beckon for more.

Hushed, the vale, draped in twilight,
Keeps its wonders hidden from sight.
Each glen and hollow, a story to tell,
Of fate and fortunes that under dwell.

Through the quiet, a soft voice calls,
Breaking through time's fragile walls.
Step lightly, dear heart, 'neath the weeping trees,
For the gloom holds the past like a lover's squeeze.

The Cradle of Moonlight and Mystery

When dusk paints the world in silvery hues,
The cradle of moonlight wakes with its views.
Stars scatter dreams like seeds in the night,
Nurtured by shadows, in soft, gentle light.

In this realm where silence pervades,
A symphony plays in the glades.
The wishes of children, cast to the sky,
In the cradle of mystery, they flutter and fly.

Crickets are singing a lullaby sweet,
While distant hoots call from branches discreet.
Beneath the starlight, secrets do weave,
In the moon's tender glow, we dare to believe.

Fingers of light thread through the dark,
Kindling the fire of an ancient spark.
Here, hearts awaken, and sorrows take flight,
In the cradle of moonlight, all feels so right.

Hidden Pathways Through the Woven Moss

Where sunlight kisses the forest's floor,
Hidden pathways lie, inviting the lore.
Moss carpets the ground, lush and so green,
In these secret trails, wonders are seen.

Stepping lightly, the world fades away,
As whispers and giggles in sunlight play.
Trees arch above with branches entwined,
Guarding the mysteries that wanderers find.

Each twist and turn, a glimpse of the past,
In these woven paths, time seems to last.
A dappled dance of shadows and light,
Leads souls in search of the purest delight.

The essence of nature, vibrant and true,
In the woven moss, the magic renews.
Explore the hidden, let your spirit soar,
For life's most profound lies just at the door.

Shadows of the Forgotten Grove

In the grove where whispers cling,
Shadows dance on the edges of night.
Ancient trees in silence sing,
Guarding stories out of sight.

Moonlight spills on hidden paths,
The air thick with secrets untold.
Echoes of forgotten laughs,
In the breeze, memories unfold.

Every thorn and every flower,
Holds the weight of those long passed.
In the stillness, magic's power,
Calls the wandering souls to last.

Beneath the boughs, the spirits roam,
With each step, the world grows still.
Calling wanderers back home,
To the echoes of their will.

So listen close and tread with care,
For the shadows know the way.
The forgotten grove is rare,
Home to dreams that gently sway.

Lullabies of Veiled Legends

In the hush of twilight's glow,
Legends weave a gentle thread.
Lullabies from long ago,
From the dreams that lovers shared.

Every note a tale unfolds,
Mysteries wrapped in soft embrace.
The night whispers, the heart beholds,
Stories hidden in twilight's grace.

Beneath the stars, the old tales sigh,
Of heroes lost and monsters slain.
In each lullaby, they lie,
Echoes of joy and of pain.

Listen closely, let them flow,
In the depths of your silent mind.
Veiled legends soft and low,
Carry your heart and soul entwined.

So close your eyes, let dreams ignite,
As lullabies of legends play.
Guiding you through the long night,
Till the dawn brings a brand new day.

Tales from the Edge of Twilight

At the edge where day must fade,
Tales are spun of light and dark.
Where the delicate dreams are made,
And mysteries leave their mark.

In the twilight's sweet embrace,
Shadows linger, stories lie.
Each whisper holds a secret place,
Where echoes of lost dreams sigh.

Time stands still as night draws near,
In the stillness, hearts take flight.
Glances shared, a hint of fear,
Tales awaken in the night.

Fables of love and ancient lore,
Come alive in crescent beams.
At the edge, they softly soar,
In the realm of fleeting dreams.

So listen close to evening's song,
For twilight holds a magic rare.
Each tale weaves us, brave and strong,
In a world beyond compare.

Night's Fabric Woven with Secrets

Beneath the veil of starlit skies,
Night's fabric shimmers, deep and thick.
Woven secrets softly rise,
In the shadows, whispers flick.

Each thread tells of hearts that yearned,
Of dreams that dared to touch the night.
In darkness, the world has turned,
To mysteries held tight in sight.

Gentle are the stories spun,
In the moon's embrace, they gleam.
As the quiet hours run,
Night unveils the waking dream.

From the depths, the spirits call,
Rising softly, drawing near.
In the dark, we are but small,
Yet worlds unfurl without fear.

Embrace the calm, the shadows beckon,
For night's fabric, rich and vast.
In its folds, the past does reckon,
Binding futures with the past.

The Mysteries Beneath the Faery Shade

Beneath the boughs where secrets cling,
Whispers weave through emerald rings.
Flickering lights like stars descend,
In twilight's embrace, the worlds blend.

Glimmers dance on a silver stream,
Echoing tales, a long-lost dream.
Faeries twirl in a gossamer haze,
Guardians of shadows in moonlit bays.

With laughter ringing through ancient trees,
Rustling leaves sing a soft reprise.
The heartbeats of night, so pure, so free,
Enfolding mysteries, wild and carefree.

Yet tread with care on this enchanted ground,
For shadows linger, and truths abound.
The faery shade holds both joy and plight,
In its woven web of radiant light.

So linger a while, let magic unfurl,
For in this realm, a new world will swirl.
Where dreams take flight and fears are laid bare,
In the mysteries found, love breathes the air.

Lurking Spirits in Dappled Light

In dappled light where wildflowers bloom,
Soft spirits linger, dispelling the gloom.
They twirl and sway with a mischievous grin,
In the hush of the forest, their dance begins.

Whispering secrets with every rustle,
Nature's wonders in a playful bustle.
Among the ferns where the shadows play,
Lurking spirits weave night into day.

Catch a glimpse of their flickering trace,
A fleeting glimpse, a moment of grace.
With laughter like echoes in the gentle breeze,
They beckon the heart, aim to please.

Yet, listen close, heed the call,
For not all that glimmers is destined to fall.
With joy comes caution, a delicate thread,
Tangled in fortune, where fates might tread.

So wander these woods with wonder anew,
In dappled light, hear the spirits' cue.
For in their presence, the world feels right,
Alive with magic, dancing in light.

Ethereal Murmurs in the Ether

In the ether swirls an ethereal song,
Threads of magic where voices belong.
Soft whispers float in a twilight embrace,
Painting the night with stars' gentle grace.

Murmurs of faeries drifting like mist,
Echoing dreams that too often twist.
Fleeting glimpses of what lies ahead,
Cloaked in the veils where the wise dare tread.

Each note holds a tale of olden days,
Of laughter and tears in the moon's silver rays.
The heartbeats of time resonate here,
With truths and wonders to cradle near.

So listen close in the quiet of night,
As whispers unravel, unveiling their light.
For in every echo, wisdom is spun,
Revealing the magic of all that's begun.

In the ethereal dance beneath the skies,
Dreams take flight, as the spirit flies.
Awake to the murmurs, let them unite,
In the sacred silence, pure and bright.

Celestial Dreams in Feyland

In Feyland's heart where dreams ignite,
Celestial wonders shimmer in the night.
Stars weave tales in a cosmic array,
Guiding lost souls on their wanderings away.

Soft echoes brush through the silken air,
Kisses of moonlight, a gentle snare.
With every twinkle, the heavens descend,
A tapestry woven that seems never to end.

Hallowed whispers from ethereal streams,
Glide through the crickets, mingling with dreams.
In this enchanted realm, where hopes ascend,
Magic is real, and the heart learns to mend.

So dance through the stardust, embrace the divine,
For in Feyland's glow, our spirits entwine.
Each promise of dawn with the stars taking flight,
Refreshes the soul in the beauty of night.

With every breath, let your spirit roam,
In celestial dreams, let your heart find home.
In the embrace of Feyland, forever be free,
As the universe sings through eternity.

The Language of Shadows and Dreams

In whispered tones, the shadows speak,
Their secrets wrapped, so bittersweet.
Lost dreams linger in the night,
A world unseen, just out of sight.

With sighs of wind on moonlit streets,
The echoes dance with quiet beats.
They weave a tale of joy and pain,
In every heart, a ghost remains.

Dare to listen, hearts will quiver,
As shadows play near the silver river.
Each sigh and whisper, a tale unfold,
In twilight's glow, where dreams are told.

With every flicker, the visions reign,
As light and dark entwine in vain.
The dance of fate in silken threads,
Awakens hopes where darkness treads.

In realms of night, where spirits roam,
The shadows sing, they call us home.
Through veils of silence, grace descends,
In dreams, we find our truest friends.

Songs of the Beneath

In caverns deep, the echoes swell,
With stories spun, they weave their spell.
Voices of old, in rhythm and song,
Carving paths where hearts belong.

The roots of earth in whispers call,
To spirits woven within the thrall.
Beneath the surface, secrets hide,
In every shadow, pulses stride.

The deep and dark, a mystic place,
Where time stands still in soft embrace.
With every note, a heartbeat's grace,
The hidden realms we dare to chase.

So listen close, for tales emerge,
From ancient ties, and quiet surge.
Through songs of light and ghostly breath,
We find our life entwined with death.

In unity, we rise and fall,
These songs of beneath, they bind us all.
In realms forgotten, truth will gleam,
As we build bridges through a dream.

The Twilight Veil and Its Guardians

As twilight falls, the veil draws near,
A whispered hush, the end is clear.
Guardians stand with watchful eyes,
In twilight's glow, where mystery lies.

With cloaks of dusk and wands of light,
They guard the realm from endless night.
With wisdom deep and hearts so bold,
In shadows dark, their stories told.

Each spirit glows with sacred fire,
Igniting dreams of lost desire.
In twilight's embrace, they weave their art,
Connecting worlds that drift apart.

The fading sun ignites the sky,
As magic flares, our spirits fly.
In shimmering hues, the guardians dance,
In twilight realms, we find our chance.

So heed the call of evening's song,
For with the night, we all belong.
In unity with shadows bright,
We rise as one, embraced by light.

Ephemeral Secrets Beneath the Stars

Beneath the stars, where dreams take flight,
Ephemeral secrets shimmer bright.
In cosmic whispers, tales unfold,
Of timeless wonders, brave and bold.

With every twinkle, a wish is cast,
A spark of hope from ages past.
The night sky weaves a silken thread,
Where dreams are born and hearts are fed.

In cosmic dance, the shadows sway,
As stardust kisses the break of day.
Secrets linger on the breeze,
In silent nights, where souls find ease.

Through galaxies, our spirits soar,
In every heartbeat, we yearn for more.
The mysteries weave through moonlit streams,
Reflecting brightly our wildest dreams.

So gaze above, let wonder flow,
In the depths of night, let magic grow.
For every star holds tales untold,
In ephemeral light, forever bold.

Shadows of Enchanted Silence

In twilight's hush, the shadows play,
Whispers weave through the fading day.
Beneath the stars, a secret sigh,
As dreams awaken, softly nigh.

A silver mist wraps ancient trees,
In every breeze, a haunting tease.
Footsteps linger where visions hide,
In enchanted silence, spirits glide.

A flicker of light, a distant call,
Echoes of magic, weaving thrall.
In moonlit glades, where secrets bloom,
Beneath the canopy, shadows loom.

With gilded dreams that softly gleam,
In every heart, a timeless theme.
Every glance hides tales untold,
In shadows deep, where night unfolds.

Embrace the dark, and let it guide,
To realms of wonder, where hopes reside.
In waltz of silence, find your peace,
As shadows dance, let worries cease.

Secrets Wrapped in Midnight Veils

Beneath the stars, the secrets hide,
In midnight veils, where dreams collide.
A silken thread, a whispered prayer,
In shadows deep, the brave may dare.

With every pulse of the night's warm breath,
Echoes of joy interlace with death.
In cloaks of dusk, the stories twine,
Wrapped in mystery, the world divine.

Crimson blooms in the stillness wait,
For lovers' touch to unveil fate.
In hushed allure, the night will sing,
Secrets await with the dawn of spring.

A shiver runs through the quiet woods,
Where every glimmer in darkness broods.
In twilight's arms, the tales unfold,
Of passions bright, and hearts of gold.

Like shadows merging at dusk's embrace,
With every glance, a tender trace.
In midnight's clasp, life finds its zeal,
Wrapped in the warmth of secrets real.

Echoes Beneath the Moonlit Canopy

In the forest deep, where shadows creep,
Echoes linger, secrets keep.
Beneath the moon's soft, glimmering gaze,
Time dances lightly through twilight's haze.

Branches whisper tales of old,
Promises in silver, stories bold.
With every rustle, the night unfolds,
A tapestry of dreams, life beholds.

Stars twinkle bright in the velvet night,
Guiding lost souls to their heart's delight.
In quiet moments, they find their way,
Echoes beneath where shadows sway.

A flicker of magic, a spark of fate,
In moonlit moments, love won't wait.
Every heartbeat, a silent plea,
Beneath the canopy, wild and free.

Glimmers of hope in the stillness rise,
Mirrored in dreams of dusky skies.
With every breath, the world feels whole,
Echoes beneath, a wandering soul.

The Darkened Veil of Dreams

In whispered realms where shadows flow,
The darkened veil begins to glow.
Each heartbeat holds a flicker's chance,
In secret worlds, the spirits dance.

With twilight's touch, the night ignites,
Invisible threads weave bold delights.
Amidst the dreams that softly creep,
Lies the magic that we keep.

Fading echoes of what once was,
The veil of dreams conceals the cause.
In secrecy wrapped, the heart prevails,
Through every whisper, the spirit trails.

Caught in the web of time's embrace,
Faces linger in a sacred space.
In silence shared, the unspoken finds,
The darkened veil of longing minds.

As dawn approaches, the shadows wane,
The essence of dreams, a lingering pain.
Yet in the light, hope starts to gleam,
Awakening souls from the darkened dream.

Lullabies of the Starlit Sea

Whispers of waves, a gentle embrace,
Moonlit reflections dance with grace.
Songs of the deep, in shadows they weave,
Cradled in dreams, the night makes us believe.

Stars twinkle softly, a lullaby's rhyme,
Waves crash in symphony, marking the time.
With every heartbeat, the tides call your name,
Lost in the rhythm, we're never the same.

Silvery shells hold secrets untold,
Beneath the dark waters, we're brave, we're bold.
Ebbing and flowing, our spirits take flight,
Guided by starlight, through the velvet night.

The lighthouse stands watch, a beacon so bright,
Guiding the wanderers back to the light.
For every lost sailor, a hope gently glows,
In lullabies sung by the ocean's sweet flows.

So close your eyes tight, feel the ocean's embrace,
Dreams ride the waves, a soft, soothing grace.
In lullabies whispered, the stories unfold,
Of starlit adventures, forever retold.

Arcane Tales Under a Silvered Sky

In shadows of magic, the whispers take flight,
Tales spun of wonders, igniting the night.
Stars painted stories upon velvet dark,
Each twinkling ember ignites a brave spark.

Wands weave enchantments in silvery beams,
The moon casts a vision, a tapestry of dreams.
Fables of courage, of love, and of loss,
Under the silver, we gather, embossed.

Charming the winds with incantations old,
A parchment, a quill, with secrets to hold.
By starlit enchantments, our destinies shift,
Under the gaze of the cosmos, we drift.

Through forests enchanted, the echoes will tell,
Of heroes and magic, of triumphs that swell.
With every heartbeat, the stories reveal,
The strength of our spirits, the bonds we can feel.

So gather your courage, let dreams take their flight,
Under the silver, let go of your fright.
In arcane tales laced with wonder and glee,
The heart of the cosmos will set our souls free.

Eclipsed Murmurs Among the Foliage

In shadows of green, where secrets reside,
Murmurs of nature in whispers abide.
Leaves brush together, a soft, gentle sigh,
Eclipsed by the twilight, where dreams softly lie.

Rabbits and foxes hold council at night,
Guided by starlight, they bask in the light.
The echoes of laughter weave through the trees,
As fireflies twinkle, a dance on the breeze.

Every rustle and hush, a tale to explore,
Old shadows linger on folklore's rich shore.
Among the tall oaks, the spirits of yore,
Whisper of magic—forever, encore.

With each ebb and flow of the cool evening air,
Nature's sweet song becomes a tender prayer.
Eclipsed by the moon, the heartbeats align,
Where whispers of wisdom through branches entwine.

So sit by the foliage, heed nature's call,
In echoes of murmurs, we find we are all.
Bound by the magic that flows in our veins,
In eclipsed serenades, our spirit remains.

Threads of Destiny in a Fae's Grasp

In the misty twilight, where legends are spun,
Threads of our fates twinkle, weave, and run.
Fae laughter echoes through shadows and light,
Guiding the dreamers who wander the night.

With delicate fingers, they pull at the seams,
Stitching our futures with hopes and with dreams.
Beneath ancient boughs, where the wildflowers dance,
We follow their magic, entranced by the chance.

Tales of enchantment twine through the air,
Each woven encounter, a fortune laid bare.
In their splendid realm, time flows like a stream,
Where wishes are gathered and spun into dream.

Moonlight aglow, like silver-threaded lace,
Binds every heart in a delicate grace.
As starlings take flight, in harmony's song,
Woven in magic, where we all belong.

So dance with the fae as the night softly sighs,
In ribbons of starlight, under velvet skies.
Threads of our fate are entwined in the past,
In the fae's gentle grasp, we find love that lasts.

Midnight Secrets in the Glade

In the hush of night, whispers play,
Beneath stars that twinkle and sway.
Ancient trees guard tales untold,
Secrets woven in shadows bold.

Moonbeams sprinkle silver light,
Dancing softly, a magical sight.
Creatures stir with gentle grace,
As dreams awaken in this place.

A breeze rustles leaves, a soft sigh,
Carrying wishes as they fly.
Mysteries linger within the air,
In the glade where magic dares.

Footsteps echo on the ground,
In this realm where hope is found.
Every heartbeat tells a story,
Of midnight secrets, fleeting glory.

So linger here, in twilight's hold,
Let the whispers make you bold.
For each night brings its own delight,
In the glade beneath the night.

Shadows Dance Beneath the Canopy

In the depths where shadows weave,
Beneath a canopy, we believe.
Twinkling fireflies paint the night,
Their soft glow, a guiding light.

Murmurs of creatures, soft and low,
Secrets shared where wild things grow.
Leaves shiver with an ancient song,
In this realm where spirits belong.

Branches twist in a graceful ballet,
As the moon begins to sway.
With every heart, a tale takes flight,
In the shadows, lost to sight.

Dancing softly, the night unfurls,
Enigmas wrapped in gentle swirls.
Each rustle holds a wish renewed,
In the dance, our dreams imbued.

Stay awhile and join the dance,
In the shadows, take your chance.
For beneath the stars, we are free,
In the magic of the canopy.

Enigmatic Echoes of the Moonlit Grove

In the grove where echoes play,
The moonlight whispers night and day.
Branches arching like a bow,
Beneath them, secrets ebb and flow.

Stars look down with knowing eyes,
Their light a veil, a thin disguise.
Each rustle tells a tale profound,
In the hush, our hearts are found.

Creatures flit with stealthy grace,
Enchantments weave in this sacred space.
A fleeting glance, a shiver direct,
In the grove, we feel the connect.

The air is thick with stories lost,
In shadows deep, we pay the cost.
With every pulse, a memory flows,
In the moonlit grove, where wonder grows.

So listen close, for wisdom's near,
In whispers soft, we hold so dear.
The echoes call, inviting our souls,
In the grove, where magic rolls.

The Veil of Night and Enchantment

A veil of night caresses the land,
Where dreams and twilight gently stand.
In shadows deep, the stars will gleam,
A tapestry woven from each dream.

Hushed whispers dance through the trees,
Carried aloft by a soft breeze.
Every sigh, a spell unspun,
In the night, all fears are done.

Moonlit paths glimmer with grace,
Every corner, a hidden place.
In this realm, lost time will bend,
An enchanting night, where stories blend.

With every step, the pulse of night,
On this journey guided by light.
Magic unfurls like petals rare,
In the silence, dreams fill the air.

So twirl with the stars, embrace the dark,
In the night, find your spark.
For beneath this veil, all things align,
In the enchantment, our hearts intertwine.

9 781805 625292